wild about you!

Adult Companion Bible Study
for Group's PandaMania VBS

Group
Loveland, Colorado
group.com

Group resources actually work!

This Group resource incorporates our R.E.A.L. approach to ministry. It reinforces a growing friendship with Jesus, encourages long-term learning, and results in life transformation, because it's

Group's R.E.A.L. GUARANTEE — RELATIONAL ★ EXPERIENTIAL ★ APPLICABLE ★ LEARNER-BASED

Relational
Learner-to-learner interaction enhances learning and builds Christian friendships.

Experiential
What learners experience through discussion and action sticks with them up to 9 times longer than what they simply hear or read.

Applicable
The aim of Christian education is to equip learners to be both hearers and doers of God's Word.

Learner-based
Learners understand and retain more when the learning process takes into consideration how they learn best.

wild about you!

Adult Companion Bible Study for Group's PandaMania VBS

Visit our website: **group.com**

This resource is brought to you by the creative team at Group Publishing.

ISBN 978-0-7644-6439-3

10 9 8 7 6 5 4 3 2   13 12 11

Printed in the United States of America.

Contents

Introducing wild about you!

Did you know that God is wild about you? Yes, *you*!

If this is a bit of a surprise, or you just need to be reminded of it on a deeper level, this is the Bible study for you. The five sessions in this study focus on Psalm 139 (where we learn how wild God is about us), and also use additional accounts from the Bible to demonstrate these truths.

PandaMania

The topics and Bible accounts in this study correspond to the five days of PandaMania. If your church is doing this amazing vacation Bible school program, *Wild About You!* is the perfect way to take adults deeper into the Bible to learn on a more mature level the same lessons their kids are exploring each day. We suggest you choose one or both of the following options for using *Wild About You!*

Very Important Pandas (Option 1)

Every day at PandaMania, parents will be stopping by to drop off their children. Instead of waving at the parents and sending them on their way, invite them to stick around and join in this Bible study!

For this option, we suggest that you invite parents to sit in the VIP (Very Important Pandas) section during the opening celebration at PandaMania. This is an area set aside for parents who want to enjoy a portion of vacation Bible school and see what their kids are learning. Parents can sit together in this area, sing along, hear what the Bible Point is for that day, and be part of the fun. Then, when children are dismissed to begin their activities, parents can join you for a time of Bible study. Include coffee and snacks, and allow time for mingling and getting to know each other better as well. Then parents can rejoin the kids in the closing celebration (again sitting in the VIP area) and be there when it's time to go home.

This option will work for parents who can only drop in for one day of Bible study, as well as for those who are able to join you every day.

PandaMania Preview (Option 2)

Many people love volunteering to serve at vacation Bible school, but wish they could be prepared with a deeper knowledge of the Bible stories kids will be exploring. Use *Wild About You!* to prepare your teen and adult volunteers and give them a thorough understanding of each day's Bible account. They'll arrive at PandaMania prepared to lead children because they've already had a chance to study each day's Scriptures ahead of time.

For this option, offer *Wild About You!* in the weeks leading up to PandaMania. You might offer this as an optional class during your Sunday school hour, or on a few weeknights in the month leading up to PandaMania. Those involved in this option will not have participated in the opening celebration of PandaMania each day, but they'll have it to look forward to during VBS!

As the Leader

You will be the only one with a copy of this book, as it's not required for each participant to have a copy. Prepare for each session by reading through the lesson, gathering any supplies needed, and praying for God to use the study to touch the hearts of those who join you. We've added tips to help you adapt the study for the needs of your group and to equip you in being a sensational leader.

Each Session

Each session includes these components:

- **Today's Focus.** This gives you a quick overview of what will be studied.
- **Bible Background.** Read this to gain new insights on the Scriptures. It will help you feel more confident as you lead the study.
- **Reflection for You.** Take time to consider the questions provided here and prepare your own heart.

- **Get Ready.** Here's where you'll find a list of supplies to gather or anything you need to do ahead of time.
- **Get Started.** This is a welcome activity to help participants get to know each other better and feel included.
- **Bible Exploration.** Here's where everyone digs into God's Word together in a meaningful way.
- **Weaving Faith Into Life.** This helps people take what they've learned and incorporate it into their daily lives.
- **With My Family.** Here's help for parents in taking the lesson and using it with their children at home. Even if participants in this study don't have children of their own, they can use this for nieces, nephews, and even friends' kids. And all your volunteers can use what they learn here as they relate to the children joining in PandaMania.
- **God Sightings.** Wrap things up by encouraging everyone to be looking for God in their day-to-day experiences. Kids will be doing this at PandaMania, and adults will want to join in as well!

We pray that this experience will help you grow as friends of Jesus and each other. Thank you for leading others in this Bible study experience. **We're wild about you, too!**

Air on coffee

Hook up computer/projector

Day 1:

God Made You

Introduction

The Bible account for Day 1 is the creation of the world, from Genesis 1, paired with Psalm 139:14 as the Bible verse for the day. These Scriptures remind us all, young and old, how special we are. God made you! No wonder he's wild about you!

Are we really THAT Good?

Entitlement

Today's Focus

Through this Bible study session, you'll help adults set aside the busyness and craziness of life for a few minutes so they can refocus their hearts and enjoy God's creation. You'll allow moments of reflection on all that God has made, and help adults see how they can discover the wonders of God's world afresh through the eyes of children. Enable people to step back from their lives, take time to consider how uniquely created each one of us is, and thank God for his role as creator of the universe.

We've also provided you with a Bible Background section to give you additional insights into the Scripture. Read it and take time to reflect.

Bible Background on Genesis 1:1–2:3

The book of Genesis gives us the beginnings. Note that this is not the beginning of God; God has existed eternally. Nor is it just the beginning of our world. It is, rather, the beginning of God's work with humans. The name *Genesis* comes from a Greek word meaning origin or beginning—and there's no better place to start than at the beginning of God's story!

Elohim is one of the Hebrew names used for God in the Old Testament. It's interesting that the name is plural, but the verb translated as *created* is singular. Even though God existed in three persons, the action of creating the universe was a unified action. One God, three persons, one plan.

Genesis 1:1–2:3 describes a vast variety of things God created, but the focus is not so much on the creation as it is on the Creator. Nine times in this passage we read, "God said" and then some variation of "It was so." God spoke our universe, our planet, and humankind into existence. And what God did was good.

The word translated as *good* here is a common Hebrew word that means "just as it should be." God looked at what he had done and knew that it was right. He didn't mess up. God knew what he was doing.

What God was doing was creating a bountiful, beautiful home for the treasured beings that he would create last. Notice that God created many of each thing: not just one tree, but "every sort of seed-bearing plant, and trees that grow seed-bearing fruit"; not just one star, but "great lights in the sky"; not just one fish, but "every living thing that scurries and swarms in the water"; not just one horse, but "all sorts of wild animals, livestock, and small animals." God prepared a marvelous earth for his crowning creation to enjoy.

And then God created humans. We are a vital part of everything good that God made.

When God finished creating the heavens and the earth and everything in them, he rested. Why? God wasn't tired. God didn't need to rest. No, God rested as a signal that Creation was complete. It became a holy day—a day to reflect on the wonder of what God had done, a day to smile and to know that it was good.

Reflection FOR YOU

God's creation is inspiring. Can you believe all he's made that we can enjoy? It's amazing! Take time to appreciate the creativity of God's design, and consider how God has designed you and your life as well. Psalm 139:14 says, "Thank you for making me so wonderfully complex!" Make this your prayer of thanksgiving today.

Get Ready

Prepare for this session by reading the entire lesson, and gather these supplies:

- ☐ several sets of iOpeners* (today you'll be using the "Fez" cards)
- ☐ Bibles
- ☐ 3 pieces of paper

*available from group.com/VBS or your Group VBS supplier

Get Started

Welcome everyone as they arrive. If you're coming from Party Time Sing 'n' Play, encourage group members to mingle and share their reactions to the excitement of this session. When you're ready to begin, have people pull their chairs together in groups of four or five. They'll stay in these groups for the remainder of this session.

Say: **Let's get to know each other a little better!**

Bring out a set of the Fez iOpener cards, and give one card to a person in each group. Have groups take a few minutes to read their card together and share their answers. Allow between 5 and 10 minutes so everyone has time to talk, then have everyone return their attention to you.

Explain that every day, children will receive these cards at PandaMania and will bring them home. Encourage adults to look at each card with their children.

Bible Exploration

Share a positive reflection about some aspect of God's creation that you enjoy or appreciate. For example, you might briefly share about a trip to the mountains or the ocean or some other natural wonder that put you in awe of God's creation. Or you might simply relate how the beauty of a flower or the sound of birds singing reminds you of God.

Invite people to add their own thoughts about God's creativity. If your class is large, have people share in their smaller groups.

Say: **The things we've mentioned are all wonderful parts of God's creation: towering mountains, delicate flowers, suns spinning in distant solar systems, and waves lapping the shores of great oceans. God spoke into existence all of Creation and sustains it all.**

We are part of God's creation too. God is a creator. But...how did the world come into existence? How did God do it? Let's start by taking a look at the Bible.

Before reading the Bible together, have everyone number off, one through six. People will stay in their existing groups, but they'll need to remember their personal number.

Say: **As we read from the Bible, we'll discover what was created on each day. Pay extra close attention to what was created on the day that corresponds to your number.**

Read Genesis 1:1–2:3 aloud together. You may want to invite someone who can read with a dramatic flair to do this.

Say: **Share in your group what God created on the day that corresponds with your assigned number, and then share something you appreciate that reflects what God created on the day you were assigned. For example, if you have the first day when God created night and day, you might share a time when you were especially impressed with a sunrise.**

Repeat the instructions if needed, and then let everyone share in their groups. Allow enough time for sharing, and then have everyone return their attention to you.

Beginning with the first day of Creation, ask someone to share his or her reflection about that day with the class. Then move to the remaining days of Creation so you have one story shared for each day of Creation.

Say: **The Bible describes God speaking matter into existence in a period of six days.**

Some Christians believe the days are literal 24-hour periods. Others believe that God measures time differently than we do, and therefore took longer to mold Creation. Some believe Creation may have begun with a God-ordained "big bang" that took many millenniums to come to fruition. Let's discuss how people reach their conclusions about Creation.

Weaving Faith Into Life

Spread out three pieces of paper on the floor in the front of the room.

Say: **These pieces of paper are "position platforms." The one on your left** (indicate this paper) **is the platform for the belief that God created the universe in six 24-hour periods. The platform on your right** (indicate this paper) **is for the position that God created the universe with a big bang and then took many years to complete the job. The platform in the middle is for any other beliefs about Creation.**

Let's get the arguments and opinions for each platform out in the open. Whether you agree with a platform or not, please step up and share what you know that is either for or against the different platforms. What are their points? Simply step onto one of these papers and take your turn speaking.

tip

What if no one steps up to share? It's OK to wait in silence, even for three minutes! Don't step in to "rescue" group members. Allow them time to gather their thoughts and then participate.

Remind everyone that this is a time of open sharing with the purpose of gathering information—not a time to attack others or belittle them.

After adults have expressed their understanding of the platforms, have them rejoin their small groups. Assign each group either John 1:3 or Colossians 1:17.

Say: **In your groups, read these verses and discuss what they add to the question of how the world came to be.**

After a few minutes, have groups share what they discovered. Then sum up.

Say: **Whatever position we take, we must be careful not to compromise at least three clear principles from the Bible:**

1. **God exists and created the heavens and the earth. (Genesis 1:1)**
2. **Without Jesus, nothing was made that has been made. (John 1:3)**
3. **Jesus sustains and supervises all that exists today. (Colossians 1:17)**

Ask:

- **How does what you believe about God creating the world impact how you feel about yourself? about others?** Lead a brief discussion on this question that involves the entire class.

Say: **Psalm 139:14 says, "Thank you for making me so wonderfully complex!" God made the world, and intentionally and complexly made each of us.**

Ask:

- **If we believe that God created not only the world, but each of us, how can our day-to-day lives reflect that?**

tip

Remind the class that it's OK if everyone doesn't agree on the same view. The goal of this discussion is not to debate how long it took to create the world, but to affirm that God did create it. Encourage open sharing and honest questioning.

With My Family

Say: **If we believe that God is a present-day creator and sustainer of life, then the children in our lives are more than the result of biology—they are God's purposeful creations. And as creations that Jesus died to save, they have a high value. Jesus didn't die to save the solar system. He died to save people—including the children we love.**

In your groups, discuss:

- **How do we help our children stand against the beliefs about creation that oppose the Bible?**
- **How can we affirm to our children that God made them to be unique, complex, and special?**

tip

Even if adults in your group are not parents, they can apply these concepts with the children they lead through your ministry and other children in their daily lives.

After a time of sharing in groups, invite a few people to share ideas they discussed in their groups with everyone.

God Sightings

Say: **Each day at PandaMania, children will be encouraged to look for God in their lives. They'll be challenged to recognize the ways God is working all around them, and they'll have opportunities to share and celebrate those ways with others.**

We want to be looking for God in our lives as well! When you leave here, I encourage you to do so with open eyes. Raise your awareness of what people are saying, doing, and feeling all around you. Look at Creation. Stop and smell the roses! Share what you see God doing with your family, and be ready to share it when you come back for our next session.

I want to remind you that God made you, too. Sometimes we're hard on ourselves and it's easy to name our flaws, but God made you with a purpose in mind. Each of you is a God sighting!

Close with a time of prayer, thanking God for making each person here a unique and complex person. Thank God for making the earth and for being such a wildly creative God.

Day 2:

God Listens to You

The Bible focus for Day 2 is the account of Elijah confronting the prophets of Baal, from 1 Kings 18, paired with Psalm 139:4 as the Bible verse for the day. These Scriptures affirm that God listens to you—no matter what you have to say!

Today's Focus

Through this Bible study session, you'll help adults remember that God is always listening, any time of the day or night. Even though many of us have heard this over and over again, it's great to stop for a few minutes and consider how incredible it is that the God who created the entire universe has time to hear us—and *wants* to hear us! This Bible account also encourages adults to find confidence in God and in their commitment to him. Not only does God *hear*, but God *acts*.

We've also provided you with a Bible Background section to give you additional insights into the Scripture. Read it and take time to reflect.

Bible Background on 1 Kings 18

During the time the prophet Elijah was staying in Zarephath, Ahab, king of Israel, was apparently looking for him. Jezebel, Ahab's wife, had been killing prophets who followed God, and we can assume Ahab and Jezebel wanted to do the same to Elijah. A man named Obadiah was in charge of Ahab's palace. Obadiah was a devout follower of God and had hidden some prophets of God from Jezebel to keep them safe.

God instructed Elijah to present himself to Ahab. The drought God caused had grown so severe that Ahab had sent Obadiah to find grass to keep his horses alive; Ahab didn't want to risk a decrease in his military strength. During his search, Obadiah encountered Elijah, and their exchange is interesting. Elijah wanted Obadiah to tell Ahab that he was coming. Obadiah was afraid to make that announcement for fear that Ahab would think he was in alliance with Elijah and kill him, especially if Elijah didn't show up. Elijah promised to keep his word, and Obadiah announced the visit to Ahab.

It's apparent that Ahab blamed Elijah for the drought. The crime Ahab accused Elijah of—being a "troublemaker of Israel"—was punishable by death (see Joshua 7:25). However, instead of ordering Elijah's execution, Ahab listened to Elijah and did what he said because Ahab was hoping Elijah would be able to end the drought.

Elijah's challenge to the prophets of Baal was intended to prove that the God of Israel is the one true God, so that the people would turn from

Baal and once again worship God. Elijah wanted to ensure that there could be no doubt of the contest's fairness, so he asked that all 850 prophets of Baal and Asherah be present to plead with their god. Before Elijah's demonstration of God's power, the people refused to commit themselves to either God or Baal (1 Kings 18:21).

Elijah stated that he was the only remaining prophet of God, but we know there were at least 100 others hidden by Obadiah. Elijah may have meant that he was the only prophet left who was willing to publicly stand up for God.

During this "showdown," Elijah began taunting the false prophets. Their response was to cut themselves, a common pagan practice in those days. People believed that injuring themselves would convince their gods that they were sincere.

When it was his turn, Elijah wanted to ensure that the contest couldn't possibly be seen as slanted in God's favor, so he had the altar and sacrifice drenched with water. Baal was thought to be the god of water and fire; Elijah wanted to show that the God of Israel is the one true God. When God responded as Elijah knew he would, the people made the right choice. With the people on his side, Elijah took advantage of the moment and got rid of the false prophets, and Ahab didn't stop him.

Reflection FOR YOU

God's power is amazing! This account reminds us of all that God controls, and even in the midst of all of this he listens to us and makes himself known to us. Take time right now to talk to God. Express what's on your heart—the ups and downs of life, the joys and concerns.

Psalm 139:4 says, "You know what I am going to say even before I say it, Lord." Even though God knows what we're going to say, he still likes to hear it from us!

Get Ready

Prepare for this session by reading the entire lesson, and gather these supplies:

- ☐ slips of paper
- ☐ sheets of paper
- ☐ pencils or pens
- ☐ colorful markers (optional)
- ☐ Bibles
- ☐ envelope
- ☐ phone book

Before everyone arrives, open a phone book to page 108 and count down to the ninth person on the page. Write that person's name and phone number on a piece of paper, and put it in a sealed envelope.

Get Started

Welcome everyone as they arrive. If you're coming from Party Time Sing 'n' Play, encourage group members to mingle and share their reactions to the excitement of this session. When you're ready to begin, have people pull their chairs together in groups of four or five. They'll stay in these groups for the remainder of this session.

Hold up the envelope you prepared ahead of time, and say that you're going to lead everyone in a fun "mind-reading" experiment. Explain that the answer will be found in this envelope at the end of the experiment.

Make sure everyone has a slip of paper and pen or pencil. Have each person write down a three-digit number that has three unique digits. Everyone will choose his or her own number. Then give these instructions for each person to follow:

1. Reverse the number, and subtract the lower number from the higher number. (For example, if the number was 653, you would reverse the number to get 356, and then subtract 356 from 653 for a result of

297.) If only two figures result from the subtraction, be sure to add a zero to the beginning, such as 079.

2. Write down the result of this equation, and then below it, reverse those numbers and add these two numbers together. (So, using the number from the example above, you would take 297 and then add 792 to that.)

3. Hand the telephone book to anyone in the group and direct him or her to look on the page indicated by the first three numbers (108) and to count down to the name indicated by the last number (9). Ask the volunteer to read aloud the name that appears at that position. Have that person then open your envelope and read aloud the answer you prepared ahead of time. Fun!

tip

The answer from this subtraction and then addition sequence will always be 1089, no matter what—but this is your secret! Don't reveal that to the group!

Say: **OK, now do you believe I'm a mind reader?** Allow everyone to laugh, and if parents want to try this math trick at home with their kids, explain the sequence again so they can remember it. Then say:

Obviously I'm not a mind reader. But God is! Psalm 139:4 is the verse we're focusing on today, and it says, "You know what I am going to say even before I say it, Lord."

Ask:

- **How do you feel, knowing that God knows *exactly* what you're going to say...even before you open your mouth? Talk about that in your groups.**

Allow a few minutes for group discussion, and then have a few people share their thoughts with the class. Then let everyone know it's time to explore the Bible to learn more about how God listens to us.

Bible Exploration

Have everyone stay in their groups. Give each person a sheet of paper, and make sure everyone has a Bible and something to write with. If you have colorful markers, this is the time to bring them out. Explain that you're going to work together in groups to make an illustrated version of an account from the Bible.

tip

Let everyone know their art is not going to be judged. Stick figures are OK!

Say: **In your groups, I'd like you to read 1 Kings 18 aloud together. You can take turns reading, or if you have someone in your group who can read with dramatic flair, invite that person to read.**

When you're done, each person will choose one section of the Bible account to illustrate. You don't have to tell others which section you're going to illustrate, and it's OK if more than one person chooses the same part of the story. Refer back to your Bibles for the details. You'll have about 15 minutes to read and then to illustrate your choice.

Allow 15 minutes for reading and drawing. Then have everyone stand up with their pictures and arrange themselves in a line in the order of the verses of 1 Kings 18. Some will have the same passage, so they can stand next to each other. When everyone is in order, turn your line into a circle so that everyone can see each other easily. If you like, you can move the chairs into a circle so participants don't have to stand for the rest of this activity.

tip

Tape the drawings to a wall or whiteboard for everyone to refer back to. Or, if you have a photocopier handy, have a volunteer make copies for anyone who wants to take a handmade "book" home to share with their children.

Begin with the person who illustrated the verses closest to the beginning of the story. Have this person show his or her artwork and tell about how it illustrates the passage, and why he or she chose this section to draw. Continue around the circle until everyone has had a chance to share.

Say: **This is a fun way to see the story unfold, and also to see which portions of this true Bible account resonate with us as adults. How do you see God listening in this account, and what difference does that listening make?**

Allow time for people to share their observations.

Say: **Now let's consider what this account means for us on a day-to-day basis.**

Weaving Faith Into Life

Have everyone return to their small groups and discuss:

- **How do these pictures help you see God's faithfulness? God's power? God's listening ear?**
- **Elijah had to listen to God instead of the outside influences of his society. What influences do you think make it challenging for your children to hear God? What influences do you think make it challenging for you to hear God?**
- **If you could draw a picture to illustrate for your children how amazing it is that God listens to them, what would you draw?**

Allow time for discussion as participants consider how this account relates to their own lives.

tip

You can help small groups move discussions along at their own pace by printing discussion questions on a white-board or sheet of news-print, and making those questions visible when you're ready for that section of the session.

With My Family

Say: **Today our kids are learning that God listens to them. And God listens to us as adults, too! How does the fact that God listens to us demonstrate that he's wild about us?**

Allow people to share their thoughts about this question.

Say: **Listening is one way God shows he's wild about us. It's also a way we can show we're wild about our kids!**

Have each person choose one item they have with them in a pocket or purse right now (like a cell phone, car keys, or even money) that distracts them from listening to their children. Ask participants to hold that item out in their open hands and share with the others in their small groups what the item represents, and how it keeps them from listening to their kids. Allow about five minutes for sharing.

Say: **I'd like you to continue to hold this item in your hand as a silent offering to God, and as a silent commitment to put this away for an hour today and listen to your child instead. Remember, God hears our thoughts, so you can silently talk to him right now; thank him for being wild about you, and ask him to help you let your kids know how wild about them you are! Let's have one minute of silent prayer.**

After one minute, say "amen" to finish this time of prayer.

God Sightings

Say: **Now it's time to share our God Sightings! I'm sure you've heard your children already talking about their God Sightings—their observations of God in their lives. Last time you were encouraged to start looking for ways that God is active in your life. Let's share what we saw!**

Allow time for people to share their God Sightings. If you have a smaller class, you can have everyone share with the entire group. If you have a larger class, have people share in their small groups.

Say: **Let's keep looking for God in our lives. Maybe next time you'll have a story to share about what it was like listening to your child or about considering the reality of God listening to you!**

Close with a time of prayer, thanking God for listening to each person in the room and for demonstrating his love through his listening ears.

Day 3:

God Watches Over You

The Bible account for Day 3 is the story of Jonah and the great fish, from Jonah 1–3, paired with Psalm 139:12 as the Bible verse for the day. These passages remind us that God watches over us no matter where we are. He's always with us!

Today's Focus

Many of us would think it's sort of creepy knowing that someone was always watching us. It might feel like we're being stalked! But today's Bible study session reminds us that God is always present with us, watching over us in a loving and protective way. As parents, it's a comfort to know God is watching over our children with even more love and care than we do ourselves, and it's also a comfort to know that even though we're grown God hasn't stopped watching over us either. He's wild enough about us to always be keeping an eye on us!

We've also provided you with a Bible Background section to give you additional insights into the Scripture. Read it and take time to reflect.

Bible Background on Jonah 1–3

Even though the story of Jonah and the "whale" (the great fish) is one of the best-known stories of the Old Testament, there are messages and fine points of this story that everyone can learn from.

Jonah's story begins within a few decades of Elisha's ministry. Israel had regained considerable strength but was being threatened by the Assyrians, whose capital was Nineveh. The Assyrians were known for their power and cruelty, and it was because of their wickedness that God commanded Jonah to preach to them (Jonah 1:2). According to classical writers, Nineveh was the largest city in the world at that time, encompassing an area about eight miles in circumference. In addition, a group of four large cities in the area was also referred to by the name Nineveh. Adding to the problem for Jonah was the likely fact that he was a very old man at the time he was called to preach to Nineveh.

Even so, apparently it wasn't fear for his own safety or the difficulty of the task that made Jonah run the other way. Instead, his reluctance was based on his knowledge of God. Jonah feared that the people of Nineveh would repent of their evil ways and that God in his compassion would forgive them. Jonah selfishly felt that the salvation of the Ninevites would not be good for his own people. He didn't want Assyria to cut in on Israel's special relationship with God.

Whether it was a great fish or a whale that swallowed Jonah is a source of debate. The truth is that we don't know for sure what it was. The Hebrew word used in the original account isn't specific. We do know that whatever it was, it was big enough to swallow Jonah and to keep him alive in its stomach for three days. Some maintain that only a sperm whale has an anatomy that would make it capable of swallowing a man.

Being swallowed by a whale would be traumatic, to say the least, but in this case the event was arranged by God to save Jonah's life. For in the belly of that whale, Jonah came to his senses and realized that he needed to obey God.

We don't know why the people of Nineveh responded so positively to Jonah's message. Perhaps God had prepared their hearts. Or maybe Jonah looked really odd after having spent three days in the digestive juices of a whale, and his story shook them up. At any rate, God spared them when they repented. We don't know exactly how long they remained repentant, but about 150 years later God exacted judgment on them again, and that time he didn't spare them.

Reflection FOR YOU

God knew what was going on in Jonah's life. From God's communication to him, to Jonah's attempt to flee God's watchful eye, to his stay inside the belly of a fish, and finally to Jonah's decision to follow God's plan—God was there, keeping an eye on Jonah the whole time. Psalm 139:12 says, "Even in darkness I cannot hide from you."

Go into a dark room and reflect on this verse for just a few minutes. Take comfort in knowing God is with you and knows what's happening in your life at every moment. What a relief!

Get Ready

Prepare for this session by reading the entire lesson, and gather these supplies:

- ☐ several sets of iOpeners* (today you'll be using the "Amanda" cards)
- ☐ Bibles
- ☐ chenille wires (the more colorful the better!)

*available from group.com/VBS or your Group VBS supplier

Get Started

Welcome everyone as they arrive. If you're coming from Party Time Sing 'n' Play, encourage group members to mingle and share their reactions to the excitement of this session. When you're ready to begin, have people pull their chairs together in groups of four or five. They'll stay in these groups for the remainder of this session.

Say: **We're halfway through the week at PandaMania, but there's so much we don't know about each other! Let's get out the iOpener cards again and learn more about each other.**

Bring out a set of the Amanda iOpener cards, and give one card to a person in each group. Have groups take a few minutes to read their card together and share their answers. Allow between 5 and 10 minutes so everyone has time to talk, and then have everyone return their attention to you.

Remind adults that every day their children are receiving these cards at PandaMania and will be bringing them home. Encourage adults to use these every day with their children.

Bible Exploration

Be sure that everyone has a Bible. Turn to Jonah and read chapters 1 through 3 aloud, using as much drama as possible. After all, this is a really dramatic event! Or if you know someone in the class who will read this with a lot of flair, invite that person ahead of time to read. (Inviting this person ahead of time will allow him or her to feel prepared and not caught off guard.)

After the account has been read, have everyone form four groups. Assign each group one of these Scripture passages: Jonah 1:1-10; Jonah 1:11-17; Jonah 2; and Jonah 3. Have groups sit together for this part of the session.

Ask each group to come up with one "pose" that they think best represents what happens in their part of the story. They'll need to all agree on the pose (think of it as a statue representing this section of Scripture), hold this pose together for a few seconds when it's time, and be ready to explain why this pose best represents what has happened in their assigned section of the Bible.

Allow groups about five to eight minutes to review their passage, create a pose, and decide why this pose best represents their verses. Then call everyone together, and have groups (beginning with the Jonah 1:1-10 group) each demonstrate their pose and explain its significance to everyone else.

After the last group has demonstrated its pose, have everyone return to their seats (in their small groups) and discuss these questions:

- **When Jonah prayed in chapter 2, what did he reveal about himself? about God?**
- **What does this whole account tell you about God?**

Allow time for groups to share together, and then move to the next section.

tip

Remind parents that this is a fun way to engage their children in Bible accounts at home. They can use this with the Jonah story later today, or with other Bible stories they share with their children.

Weaving Faith Into Life

Say: **God was watching over Jonah, the sailors, the people of Nineveh, and everyone else in this account. He had a plan and was keeping an eye on things to make sure his plan was completed. It may not have seemed like it at the time, but God was right there. Take time in your groups to share about a time you felt that God was watching over you, even if the situation was difficult, and tell what you experienced of God's watchful care.**

Allow time for everyone to talk in their groups, likely about 10 minutes.

Say: **Psalm 139:12 reminds us, "Even in darkness I cannot hide from you." Jonah discovered this to be true, and many of us have realized the truth of this verse in our own lives as well.**

Even though Jonah had disobeyed, God was there watching over him, and God was still wild about Jonah! God was also wild about those Ninevites, and really wanted them to repent and turn to him, so he was watching over Jonah to make sure that happened.

As parents, we carefully watch our children and sometimes see them do something they shouldn't. During those times our kids probably wish we weren't watching! Do you ever wish God wasn't watching you? Why or why not? You don't have to share your thoughts aloud, but think about that for a moment in silence.

Allow a minute of reflection.

With My Family

Say: **We can take comfort in knowing that even though we can't be there every moment to watch over our kids, God is always there and knows what's happening in their lives.**

Give each person a chenille wire. Explain that you'd like each person to shape a pair of "eyeglasses" from the wire. If you have extra wire, people can make silly or goofy glasses if they'd like. When everyone is done, say:

Take these with you and put them in a place you'll see them every day for at least a week. On a dresser, hanging from a mirror, inside the refrigerator...wherever you know you'll see them every day for a week. It would be great if you put them in a place where your children could also see them.

Then, every time you see them, thank God for watching over you and for watching over your children. Thank him for being so wild about all of you that he cares enough to be there with you, no matter where you are. Let your kids know what the glasses are there for, so they'll know you're wild about them and are praying with them in mind each day.

God Sightings

Say: **Now it's time to share our God Sightings! Last time I encouraged you to be looking for ways that God is active in your life. Let's share what we saw!**

Allow time for people to share their God Sightings. If you have a smaller class, you can have everyone share with the entire group. If you have a larger class, have people share in their small groups.

Say: **Let's keep looking for God in our lives. Maybe next time you'll have a story of being aware of God watching over you or someone you love. Be ready to share again as we celebrate the ways God is at work in our lives every day.**

Close with a time of prayer, thanking God for watching over each person, and asking God to bring comfort during those times we feel alone.

Day 4:

God Loves You, No Matter What

The Bible account for Day 4 is of Jesus' death and resurrection, from Luke 22–24, along with Psalm 139:24 as the verse for today. Nothing could show God's wild love for us in a more amazing way than his death on our behalf, and the gift to us of everlasting life.

Today's Focus

Many people today believe their sins are "no big deal"—a lie, an unkind word, or ignoring the rules now and then. Others may feel like their sins are too big to ever be forgiven—bullying, swearing, or abuse. In God's eyes, sin is sin; there is no big and no little. Every sin hurts our relationship with him. That's why God sent his precious Son to be the perfect sacrifice to pay for every sin. The focus of today's study is that God loves us in spite of our sin, and that Jesus' death and resurrection paid for *all* the wrong things we do.

We've also provided you with a Bible Background section to give you additional insights into the Scripture. Read it and take time to reflect.

Bible Background on Luke 22:31–24:12

Pilate, the Roman governor of Judea, had been less than pleasant to the Jews during his rule. He had taken money from the temple treasury for a city water project and had brought images from the Roman Empire into the city of Jerusalem. But he knew not to go too far in irritating the Jews. If too many complaints about him reached Rome, he might lose his position. So he was likely feeling insecure when the Jews came to him with their request to crucify Jesus. Thus, even though it appears that Pilate felt Jesus was innocent, he was unwilling to stand up against the Jews. Against his better judgment, he granted their wish and sent Jesus to be crucified.

It is significant that Jesus was crucified between two criminals. To the Jews, this indicated that he was a criminal. It seems likely that the religious leaders had exerted their influence to arrange for this positioning as one more way to humiliate Jesus.

The centurion mentioned in Luke 23:47 was a Roman soldier, loyal to the emperor. Something about what happened as Jesus died made a difference in that man's life. Jesus was a righteous man who died for the sins of all who believed. But thanks to God, the story doesn't end in death.

When the women saw the two men at the tomb, their response was one of fear and respect, as indicated by their facedown posture. We don't know why the women and the disciples didn't seem to remember Jesus' predictions that he would be killed and then raised again on the third day (Matthew 16:21). However, the angels' statement reminded them of those words.

The report of the women was not enough to convince the disciples that Jesus was alive. Peter and John, according to John 20:3, ran to the tomb to see for themselves. And even after Peter had seen the empty tomb, he was confused and didn't yet believe Jesus had arisen.

tip

It is very possible that there will be adults in your group who have not heard the message of grace and forgiveness that you're going to explore today, and who don't know what it means to have a relationship with Jesus. Be prepared to share your own story with these people and guide them to the truth of God's love and salvation.

Reflection FOR YOU

The pain, suffering, and death that Jesus went through so that we could have a relationship with God is beyond our imagination. Yet he loves us that much! He loves *you* that much! No matter what you do, God loves you.

How is what Jesus did for you reflected in your life? How do others know that you've been touched by the love and grace of Jesus? Think about it.

Get Ready

Prepare for this session by reading the entire lesson, and gather these supplies:

- ☐ photocopies of the station instructions (located at the end of this lesson)
- ☐ Bibles
- ☐ pens
- ☐ index cards
- ☐ adhesive bandages
- ☐ several small pillows
- ☐ bright light or lamp with an exposed bulb
- ☐ several nails

You'll be setting up five different "stations" for prayer and reflection. The easiest way to do this is to place five tables (card tables will work fine) around the room where people can move around them easily. Photocopy the station instructions located at the end of this lesson.

Then:

1. On table 1, place the Luke 22:31-34 instructions and the index cards.

2. On table 2, place the Luke 22:54-62 instructions and the adhesive bandages.

3. On table 3, place the Luke 23:1-25 instructions and the pillows.

4. On table 4, place the Luke 23:32-47 instructions and the nails.

5. On table 5, place the Luke 24:1-12 instructions and the bright light.

Get Started

Welcome everyone as they arrive. If you're coming from Party Time Sing 'n' Play, encourage group members to mingle and share their reactions to the excitement of this session. When you're ready to begin, have everyone find a place to sit.

Say: **Have you ever heard of silly laws that different states, cities, or counties have? Some have just been around for a long time and never updated, and others apparently had a reason to be made into laws at one time, but seem crazy to us today. Let's see if we have any lawbreakers in our group.**

Have everyone stand. As you read these silly laws from various parts of the United States, anyone who has broken that law must sit down. See who can remain standing the longest.

In some parts of the United States it is illegal...

- **to play dominoes on Sunday.**
- **for women to wear shoes with sharp, high heels.**
- **to buy or sell blue lightbulbs.**
- **for dogs to bark after 6 p.m.**
- **to set a mouse trap without a hunting license.**
- **for women to wear pants.**
- **to allow a dandelion to grow within city limits.**
- **not to own a rake.**

Congratulate anyone left standing on his or her remarkable ability to abide by the laws!

Say: **Even if these laws seem ridiculous or outdated, there's no question that all of us have sinned in life. Not one of us has lived a perfect and blameless life. But God still loves us and is wild about us. He loves us so much that he allowed Jesus to take the punishment we deserve for our sins so that we could have a relationship with God and have everlasting life. Today we're going to look more closely at the events surrounding Jesus' death and resurrection as we consider that God loves us, no matter what.**

Bible Exploration *and* Weaving Faith Into Life

Be sure that everyone has a Bible and a pen.

tip

Today's session combines the Bible Exploration and Weaving Faith Into Life sections into one longer section where everyone will explore the Bible account and consider how it applies to their personal lives.

Say: **We're going to take a more reflective approach to our Bible Exploration today, but before we begin I'm going to give a short overview of the Scriptures we'll cover.**

Peter, one of Jesus' closest friends and followers, proclaims his eternal loyalty to Jesus, even to the point of death, but Jesus says that Peter will deny him three times before the rooster crows the next day. After this, Jesus and his followers go to a garden to pray. While Jesus is praying, his followers fall asleep. A crowd comes into the garden, and another of Jesus' followers, Judas, betrays him and hands him over to the guards.

Jesus is arrested. While waiting around to see what happens, Peter three times denies knowing Jesus; just as Jesus had predicted, the rooster then crows. During this time Jesus is beaten and mocked by the guards. He is then judged by the local leaders who don't have any real reason to punish Jesus, but the religious leaders put pressure on them to put Jesus to death, so he is sentenced to be crucified.

Jesus is nailed to a cross and left there to die. He is crucified alongside two criminals, one of whom turns his heart to Jesus at this time. Jesus dies and is placed in a tomb. On Sunday morning women come to his grave to anoint his body with spices. Instead of Jesus' body, they find dazzling angels who tell them Jesus has risen from the dead!

Now that you've given the brief overview, you'll give instructions for the time of Bible exploration and reflection.

Say: **Around the room are various stations. On each table you'll find instructions for that station along with an item or items that you'll use there. You can do these stations in any order you like.**

Be sure everyone understands the instructions, and then have people choose a place to begin and move around the room to the stations at their own pace. Allow about 20 minutes for this experience, or longer if you have time. Give a "you have two minutes left" warning near the end of the allotted time so people can finish the station they are at. If someone doesn't have time to complete all the stations, that's OK.

When your time is up, have everyone sit in groups of four. Have people share in their groups one thing that was personally meaningful to them during the time of reflection. Allow about 10 minutes for sharing, and then say:

tip

Playing music softly in the background while people move about the room will help create a more peaceful and reflective mood.

Jesus died on the cross and came back to life to pay the penalty for our sins. He took the punishment for us because he loves us so much!

With My Family

Have everyone discuss these questions in their small groups:

- **What does God's forgiveness and unending love mean to you personally? What does it mean to you as a parent?**
- **Psalm 139:24 says, "Lead me along the path of everlasting life." How does this verse relate to the Bible account we've explored today? How is God leading you? How are you following?**

After a time of discussion, ask groups to pray together, praying for each other and for the children in each family to come to know God's everlasting and gracious love.

God Sightings

Say: **Now it's time to share our God Sightings! Let's share what we we've experienced since we were together last!**

Allow time for people to share their God Sightings. If you have a smaller class, you can have everyone share with the entire group. If you have a larger class, have people share in their small groups.

Say: **Let's keep looking for God in our lives. Be ready to share again next time as we celebrate the ways God is at work in our lives every day.**

Close with a time of prayer, thanking God for being so wild about us that he gave his Son for us. Ask God to help each person extend that kind of love and grace to others.

1

- Read **Luke 22:31-34** in your Bible.

- Peter made a huge promise here. Think about a time you made a big promise. Perhaps it was one that has been difficult to keep.

- On an index card write "I promise" and sign your name. Let this represent the commitment you are thinking of.

- Reflect on what it means to make a commitment like this. What challenges are making this promise difficult to keep? Ask God to help you stay true to this commitment.

- Tuck your index card into your Bible as a reminder to turn to God for help in keeping your promises.

wild about you!

2

wild about you!

- Read **Luke 22:54-62** in your Bible.
- Peter had promised to follow Jesus even to death, but within hours he denied he even knew Jesus. He hurt someone he loved, and as soon as he realized it he wept with regret.
- Think about a time you hurt someone through your words or actions and later regretted it.
- Open an adhesive bandage and write the name of the person you hurt on that bandage. Place the bandage on the back of one of your hands as a reminder of the suffering your actions caused.
- Ask God to forgive you for hurting the person you named. Ask God to help you forgive yourself.
- Wear the bandage until you've had a chance to ask the person you hurt for forgiveness. When that happens, throw that bandage away!

3

wild about you!

- Read **Luke 23:1-25** in your Bible.

- Even though Pilate didn't find Jesus guilty of any crime, he was pressured to sentence Jesus to death.

- Pick up a pillow and squeeze it. Remember a time you felt pressured to do something against your better judgment. Consider times you still feel "squeezed" to do things you don't believe are right.

- Tell God about your feelings. Ask him for strength to resist the squeezing pressures.

- Give the pillow a squeeze again, this time as a reassurance that God's presence is around you, holding and comforting you. Remember this squeeze of reassurance the next time you feel pressured to go against what is right.

4

wild about you!

- Read **Luke 23:32-47** in your Bible.

- Pick up one of the nails and gently press it against your skin. Feel the sharpness and the threat of pain. Consider the pain that Jesus suffered on your behalf. What does this mean to you?

- Many parents are willing to endure pain or discomfort so that their children can find more enjoyment in life. Think about a time you didn't get something you needed for yourself so your child could have what he or she needed, or a time you went through a painful experience to help your child or someone else you love mature. Pray for that person you sacrificed for, asking God to continue to show his love to that person.

- Now think about someone who has suffered pain on your behalf. Consider how you could thank this person or show your appreciation in the near future. Thank God that he has placed people in your life who are willing to go through something difficult with you or for you.

- Thank God for the pain he endured for you. Ask God to give you strength for the painful moments in life that will be ahead.

5

- Read **Luke 24:1-12** in your Bible.

- Look at the brightness of the light before you—but don't stare too long or you'll hurt your eyes! The women in the Bible account were dazzled by the bright light of the angels, even to the point of fear. This was an amazing and unexpected turn of events!

- Remember a time you were surprised or dazzled by the actions of someone else. Reflect on those feelings. Joy? Delight? Or fear? What does it take to make you feel these emotions?

- Consider the amazing, surprising, and dazzling things Jesus has done for you. Take a quick glance back at that bright light as you remember those things. Praise God for all the bright and awesome things he's done!

wild about you!

Day 5:

God Gives Good Gifts

The Bible account for Day 5 is of God giving Hannah a baby, from 1 Samuel 1–2, paired with Psalm 139:5 as the day's verse. These passages remind us that God gives good gifts. Why? Because he's wild about us!

Today's Focus

We've explored so many different ways God shows us he's wild about us, from creating us, to watching over us and listening to us, to even sending his Son as a sacrifice for us. It seems we couldn't want for any more! But God goes above and beyond, giving us good gifts simply because of his love for us. Today we'll look at the gift God gave Hannah as a reminder that he gives us good gifts today, gifts that demonstrate his love and that continue his plans and purposes.

We've also provided you with a Bible Background section to give you additional insights into the Scripture. Read it and take time to reflect.

Bible Background on 1 Samuel 1:1–2:11

To understand the pain caused by Hannah's childlessness, one must realize how important it was in Old Testament times that women provide children. A woman who couldn't conceive was an embarrassment, or even a disgrace, to her husband. Men needed an heir to inherit the family name and property and to care for the parents in their old age.

Adding to Hannah's pain were the taunts of Elkanah's other wife, Peninnah, a situation that illustrates the strife that the practice of polygamy can create. Even Elkanah's love for Hannah and his words of encouragement could not comfort her.

Hannah poured out her heart—even her bitterness—to God. Her prayer was so anguished that Eli, the priest, assumed she was drunk! God wants to hear from us when we're hurting. We can go to him with our problems and needs.

Hannah's prayer and God's answer to it included her vow that if God gave her a son, she would give him fully to the service of the Lord.

When Samuel was born, Hannah lived up to her vow. Sometime after Samuel was about three years old, Hannah took him to Eli at the tabernacle and handed him over to be raised by the priest in service to the Lord. Samuel's name is also significant to Hannah's experience, as it means "heard of God."

God commanded the Israelites to worship at the tabernacle three times a year, at specific festivals: the Festival of Unleavened Bread, the Festival of Harvest, and the Festival of the Final Harvest. The tabernacle at Shiloh was about 16 miles from Elkanah's home.

Reflection FOR YOU

In this account Hannah cried out in hurt and sadness. God heard her and responded with a long-awaited child for her. God responds to us in different ways, but he always hears us.

How has God responded to you when you've cried out to him? What sadness do you need to leave with God right now? It's great to know we serve a God who cares about our human hurts. As Hannah did, pour out your heart to God and let him touch your life with his grace.

Get Ready

Prepare for this session by reading the entire lesson, and gather these supplies:

- ☐ several sets of iOpeners* (today you'll be using the "Lulu" cards)
- ☐ Bibles
- ☐ paper
- ☐ pens

*available from group.com/VBS or your Group VBS supplier

Get Started

Welcome everyone as they arrive. If you're coming from Party Time Sing 'n' Play, encourage group members to mingle and share their reactions to the excitement of this session. When you're ready to begin, have people pull their chairs together in groups of four or five. They'll stay in these groups for the remainder of this session.

Say: **It's our last day of PandaMania, but there's still time to get to know each other better! Let's get out the iOpener cards again and learn more about each other.**

Bring out a set of the Lulu iOpener cards, and give one card to a person in each group. Have groups take a few minutes to read their card together and share their answers. Allow between 5 and 10 minutes so everyone has time to talk, then have everyone return their attention to you.

Encourage adults to use these with their children.

Bible Exploration

Say: **We're going to read about a woman named Hannah and what God did in her life. As you listen to this account, try to put yourself in Hannah's place. What do you think her life was like? What would you have done if you were her? Think about these questions as you hear the story.**

Read 1 Samuel 1:1–2:11 aloud, or have a volunteer read it aloud. Encourage others to follow along in their own Bibles. Then have everyone discuss these questions with their groups. If time permits, have a few people share their thoughts with the larger group before moving to the next question.

- **As you put yourself in Hannah's shoes, what were you thinking? What was her life like? What would you have done if you were her?**
- **Why do you think Hannah couldn't be happy with just the love of her husband?**
- **It appears that Hannah didn't lash out at Peninnah. What does this tell us about Hannah? What would you have done or said if you had been in this situation?**
- **What do you learn about God from this account?**

Allow time for discussion, and then move to the next section.

Weaving Faith Into Life

Say: **God heard Hannah and responded by giving her the gift of a child. A lot of times we focus on the difficulties of life and forget to look for the good things that God has done for us, the good gifts he's given us. Having the God Sightings challenge each day has likely made each of us more aware of God working around us, but it's still important to stop regularly and thank God for the wonderful gifts he's given us.**

Give each person a sheet of paper and a pen. Explain that everyone has two minutes to list as many good gifts from God as possible. Time for two minutes. Then have a short time of "popcorn" prayer, where you begin by saying, "Lord, we know you're wild about us, and we're wild about you! We thank you for..." and everyone simply calls out items from their list, sort of like popcorn popping up. Let people pray in thanksgiving and praise for a few minutes, and then close with "amen."

With My Family

Say: **Our verse today is Psalm 139:5, which says, "You place your hand of blessing on my head." In our families it's possible that when we're placing a hand on our children, it's not in blessing. But this is an important part of being an effective parent—blessing your children.**

This may feel a little odd, but we're going to practice putting a hand of blessing on someone else, so that when we get home with our family members we can be ready to place a hand of blessing on them as well.

Have everyone stand in a circle, with each person facing the back of the person in front of them. Ask participants to each put a hand on the head or shoulder of the person in front of them. Have everyone say aloud (in turns or in unison), "I place a hand of blessing on you." Then allow about one or two minutes of silent prayer, with each person praying for the person he or she is touching. Then have everyone return to their small groups and discuss:

- **How did you feel blessing someone else? Being blessed by someone else?**
- **What does it mean to you that God puts a hand of blessing on your head? How does it relate to God's wild love for you?**
- **What could it mean to your children or other family members if you would put a hand of blessing on their heads each day and speak words of affirmation, of encouragement, words from the Bible, or words of prayer? What might happen if you did this?**

Encourage everyone to take this verse seriously, both as they receive the blessing God has for them, as well as when they bless others.

God Sightings

Say: **This is our last day to share God Sightings together! I encourage you to keep looking for God in your life at all times, and keep finding others to share those God Sightings with!**

Allow time for people to share their God Sightings. If you have a smaller class, you can have everyone share with the entire group. If you have a larger class, have people share in their small groups.

Say: **Let's keep looking for God in our lives. And share these with your families and friends!**

Close with a time of prayer, thanking God for the time you've had together, for the good gifts he gives, and for his hand of blessing. And most of all, thank God for being wild about every person in this room!

tip

If you've enjoyed sharing God Sightings with each other, consider using the *God Sightings™ One-Year Companion Guide* and *God Sightings One-Year Small Group Leader Guide* to continue your time together. Or start a new group with God Sightings! Find out how to do this as a personal study, as a group study, or even as a whole-church program at mygodsightings.com. Download free samples, hear stories from others, and more!

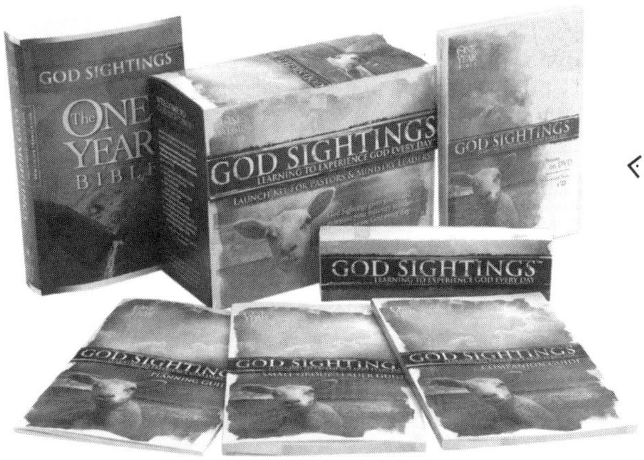